To parents and teachers

We hope you and the children will enjoy reading this story in either English or Spanish. The story is simple, but not *simplified,* so the language of the Spanish and the English is quite natural but there is lots of repetition.

At the back of the book is a small picture dictionary with the key words and how to pronounce them. There is also a simple pronunciation guide to the whole story on the last page.

Here are a few suggestions on using the book:

- Read the story aloud in English first, to get to know it. Treat it like any other picture book: look at the pictures, talk about the story and the characters and so on.

- Then look at the picture dictionary and say the Spanish names for the key words. Ask the children to repeat them. Concentrate on speaking the words out loud, rather than reading them.

- Go back and read the story again, this time in English *and* Spanish. Don't worry if your pronunciation isn't quite correct. Just have fun trying it out. Check the guide at the back of the book, if necessary, but you'll soon pick up how to say the Spanish words.

- When you think you and the children are ready, you can try reading the story in Spanish only. Ask the children to say it with you. Only ask them to read it if they are eager to try. The spelling could be confusing and put them off.

- Above all encourage the children to have a go and give lots of praise. Little children are usually quite unselfconscious and this is excellent for building up confidence in a foreign language.

First edition for the United States and Canada published 1994 by Barron's Educational Series, Inc.
Text © Copyright 1994 by b small publishing, Surrey, England

All rights reserved. No part of this book may be reproduced in any form, by photostat, microfilm, xerography, or any other means, or incorporated into any information retrieval system, electronic or mechanical, without the written permission of the copyright owner.

Address all inquiries to: Barron's Educational Series, Inc., 250 Wireless Boulevard, Hauppauge, New York 11788

International Standard Book Number 0-8120-6452-6   Library of Congress Catalog Card Number 94-2433

Printed in Hong Kong   19 18 17 16 15 14 13 12 11 10

Goodnight everyone

Buenas noches a todos

Lone Morton
Pictures by Jakki Wood
Spanish by Rosa Martín

BARRON'S

"Bedtime, Martha," called Mom.
"Yes Mom, we're almost ready,"
replied Martha.

"A la cama, Marta," dijo mamá.
"Sí mamá, ya casi estamos listos,"
respondió Marta.

"Monkey, you go there," said Martha,
"then you ... teddy,

"Tú, monito, te pones allí," dijo Marta,
"ahora tú ... osito,

and you two penguins,

y ustedes, mis dos pingüinos,

and you, baby rabbit.

y tú, conejito.

Shouldn't forget you, big gorilla,
and you panda,

No me olvido de ti, mi gran gorila,
ni de ti, oso panda,

and rag doll Anna,

y Ana, mi muñeca,

and you three...
mouse, lamb, and snake ...

y ustedes tres...
el ratón, el cordero y la serpiente ...

and elephant.

y el elefante.

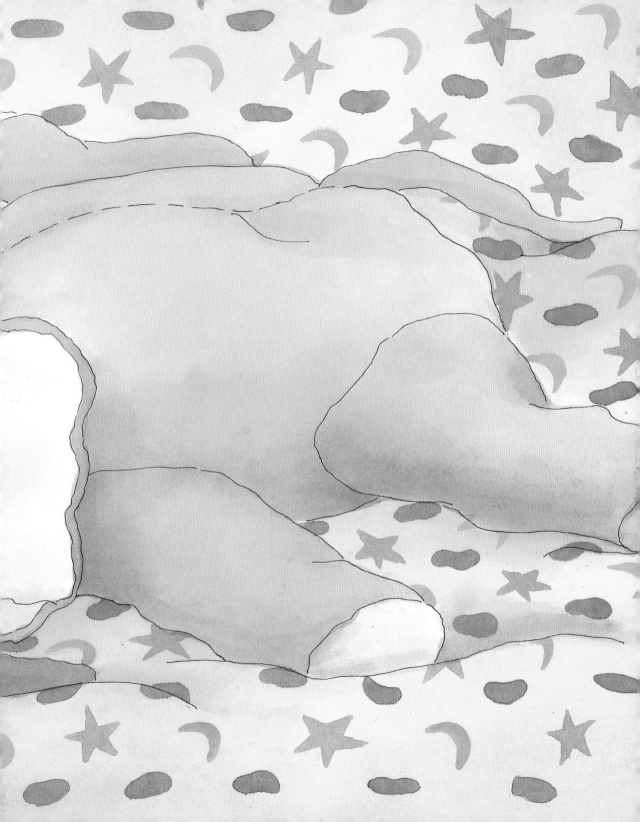

Oh, and I'll put my books here,
and my clock next to my pillow,
and my slippers by my bed."

Oh, y aquí pondré mis libros,
y mi despertador al lado de la almohada,
y mis zapatillas al lado de la cama."

"Are you ready yet?" asked Mom.
"Yes," said Martha.
"But where will *you* sleep, Martha?"

"¿Estás lista?" preguntó mamá.
"Sí," dijo Marta.
"Pero, Marta, ¿dónde vas a dormir *tú*?"

"In bed with them."
"Like this!" said Martha.

"En la cama, con ellos.
¡Así!" dijo Marta.

"Well, goodnight Martha
and goodnight everyone," said Mom.

"Bueno, buenas noches, Marta,
y buenas noches a todos," dijo mamá.

"Sweet dreams!"

"¡Que duermas bien!"

Pronouncing Spanish

Don't worry if your pronunciation isn't quite correct. The important thing is to be willing to try. The pronunciation guide here is based on the Spanish accent used in Latin America. Although it cannot be completely accurate, it certainly will be a great help.

• Read the guide as naturally as possible, as if it were English.

• Put stress on the letters in *italics*, e.g., o*sito*.

If you can, ask a Spanish-speaking person to help and move on as soon as possible to speaking the words without the guide.

Words Las palabras

lass pal-*abrass*

(little) monkey
el monito

el mon-*eeto*

teddy
el osito

el o*seeto*

penguin
el pingüino
el ping*wee*no

panda
el oso panda
el *osso* *pan*da

rabbit
el conejo
el con*ay*-ho

mouse
el ratón
el rat-*on*

gorilla
el gorila
el go*reel*a

lamb
el cordero
el cor*dairo*

snake
la serpiente
lah sairp-*yenteh*

clock
el despertador
el despairtad-*dor*

book
el libro
el *lee*bro

elephant
el elefante
el eleh-*fanteh*

pillow
la almohada
la almo-*hada*

bed
la cama
lah *cam*ma

doll
la muñeca
lah moon*yek*kah

slipper
la zapatilla
lah sapa*tee*-ya

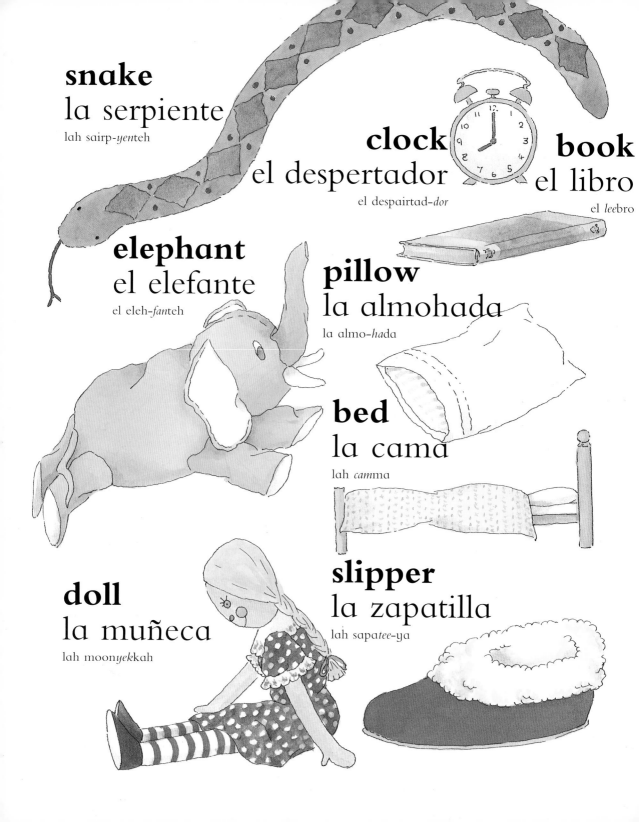

A simple guide to pronouncing this Spanish story

Buenas noches a todos
*bwen*nass *noch*ess a *tod*dos

"A la cama, Marta," dijo mamá.
ah lah *cam*ma, *Mar*-ta, *dee*-ho mam*ma*

"Sí mamá, ya casi estamos listos," respondió Marta.
see mam*ma*, ya *cah*-see es*tam*mos *lees*toss, respondee-*oh* *Mar*-ta

"Tú, monito, te pones allí," dijo Marta,
too, mon-*ee*to, teh *pon*ess a*yee*, *dee*-ho *Mar*-ta

"ahora tú ... osito,
ah-*ora* too ... os*ee*to

y ustedes, mis dos pingüinos,
ee oos-*teh*dehs meess doss pin-*gwee*noss

y tú, conejito.
ee too conay-*hee*to

No me olvido de ti, mi gran gorila,
noh meh ol*vee*do deh tee, mee gran gor*ee*la

ni de ti, oso panda,
nee deh tee, *os*so *pan*da

y Ana, mi muñeca,
ee Ana, mee moon-*yek*ka

y ustedes tres ...
ee oos-*teh*dehs tress

el ratón, el cordero y la serpiente...
el rat-*on*, el cord*air*o ee la sairp-*yen*teh

y el elefante.
ee el eleh-*fan*teh

Oh, y aquí pondré mis libros,
o, ee a*kee* pond-*reh* meess *lee*bross

y mi despertador al lado de la almohada,
ee mee despairtad-*dor* al *lad*do deh lah almo-*add*a

y mis zapatillas al lado de la cama."
ee meess sapa*tee*-yass al *lad*do deh la *cam*ma

"¿Estás ya lista?" preguntó mamá.
es*tass* ya *lees*ta? pregoon*to* mam*ma*

"Sí," dijo Marta.
see, *dee*-ho *mar*ta

"Pero, Marta, ¿dónde vas a dormir tú?"
*per*ro, *mar*ta, *don*deh vass a dor*meer* too?

"En la cama, con ellos."
en la *cam*ma, con *el*-yoss

"¡Así!" dijo Marta.
as*see*! *dee*-ho *mar*ta

"Bueno, buenas noches, Marta,
*bwen*no, *bwen*nass *noch*ess, *mar*ta

y buenas noches a todos," dijo mamá.
ee *bwen*nass *noch*ess a *tod*dos, *dee*-ho mam*ma*

"¡Que duermas bien!"
keh *dwer*mass b-*yen*